In a World of Black and *W*hite

© Charles R Haffner 2024
ALL RIGHTS RESERVED

ISBN: 9780796185006

Presents
In a World of Black and White
By
Charles R Haffner

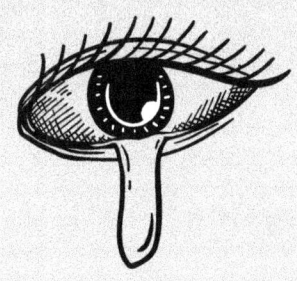

In a world of black and white is a book about the author's views of depression. From the loss of his parents and a twenty six year marriage ending in divorce. In micropoetry we explore the roots Of the silent killer. Depression.

Charles R Haffner

Charles R. Haffner is a poet and author who has written several books of poetry, including "Orchids under the Stars: Seasonal Tanka poetry" and "A Gator and a Bunny Chow: A collection of Senryu poetry" ¹. He was born and raised in Baltimore, Maryland, and now resides in Durban, South Africa.

For Elizabell and Max.
Thank you for letting me be me.

Rooster and an ox
Play with a German shepherd.
He loves them dearly.

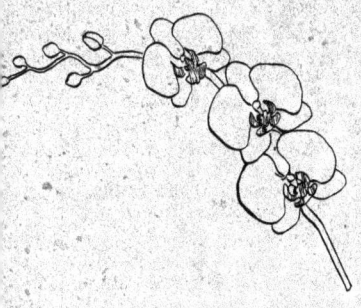

Precious gift arrives.

Protected.

Introducing earth.

Where were you all of those restless nights?
As the stars filled the night sky,
I wondered if each represented a white lie.
A something so little couldn't affect anyone's life.

No more happiness is in sight.
A mother tries to help her child with all her might.
A weary soul experiences pain in life.
A smile lost from many years of pain.
The tears that flow are invisible in rain.
Nothing will ever be the same.
Since my heart knows I am the one to blame.

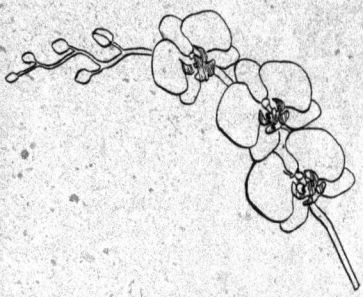

A cloud gives a waking bear a good morning wave.
As the grumpy old thing walks out the cave.
Sweaty old hands push a broom from room to room.
After the snows melt and the first flowers bloom.
The finger that points is only aimed at you.
No more cheer or grace just solitude.
Years lost hiding your only face.
Is it really worth the damn chase?

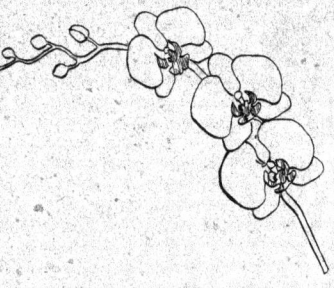

Where are you now? Where is the place that no one sleeps?

A memory where pain hides and dreams speak.

A rusty part of my brain that is afraid of defeat.

Wrapped in many layers when fear shows itself.

Almost like when a hand pushes an envelope.

Floating past children trying to escape.

A flea wants to join a circus.

Watching a pope eating his frosted flakes.

A chain of gold wrapped around a neck

Of a person you want to punch in the face.

I scream for the joy of hearing that I brought this ruin.

I wish I could explain myself better.
I wish for the sun after rain.
I wish the time was better spent.
I wish to see this every time I see the waves.

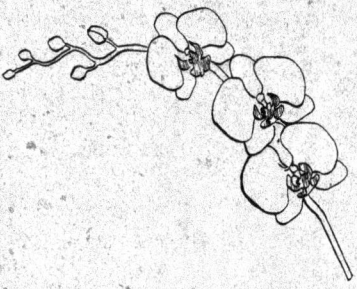

Why must I carry on?

What purpose is holding a heavy heart?

Why do I have to stand back?

What is waiting for me?

That keeps my mind stuck in its own misery?

I wished for the stars, but
Could not climb the stairs.
I wanted kindness to make things better.
I wasted many years of youth.
Staring at stairs leading to heaven.
Afraid of the incline, since I saw no railings.

I wanted to be normal like everyone else.
A family and a house with a white picket fence.
A chance to love with maybe children.
A job to support me like a skeleton.
The memories of life that is pleasant.
Instead of the dread of this present.

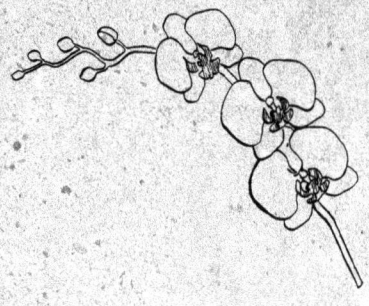

I gaze at what has become our world.
A dying ember of a fiery garden.
A child that tries to run, but keeps falling.
A place that people exagerate their worth.
A place where you are mocked since your birth.
A time where the only feeling is hurt.

It is ok to never get over the loss.
They were an ispiration since the start.
In your life they were a huge part.
A support system of various words.
A love so strong it could always be heard.
Now that system has gone to bed.
Now your heart wishes it was dead.

Our voices are just like the dead.
Carefully sewn lips with the finest silk thread.
Miniscule as ancient piles of dust.
Hidden away close to the earth's crust.
Lost whispers in a valley before dusk.

I remember some first days.
Pink ribbons in their hair.
A smile that you couldn't bear.
A time when you lived with out a care.
Visions we carry everynight in our sleep.
A time when the pit you have dug is too deep.
A thoughtless moment before we sleep.

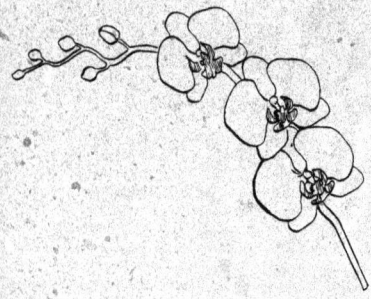

Where has the time gone?

Why do I still have the will to move on?

Hope is my only enemy when I sleep.

It presents shows to remind me that I am weak.

Giving me an ego that can never be meek.

A dream is never possible with open eyes

For you realize that only time truly flies.

How do I finally move on?

Now that I know where all the precious time has gone?

What brought your world over to me?

Why are you the only person that tries to make me happy?

When will my soul finally break free?

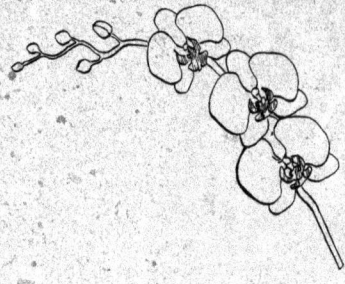

A family lost to only one brother.
A coffee table with a picture of a mother and father.
A vase on a table that no one bothers.
A dreary rain silently plays on a lanai.
A child asks their parent why do people die?
The parent could only lie, since every heart will eventually cry.

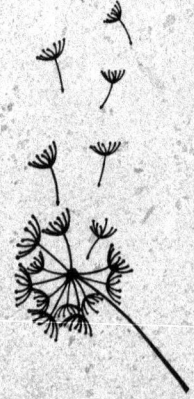

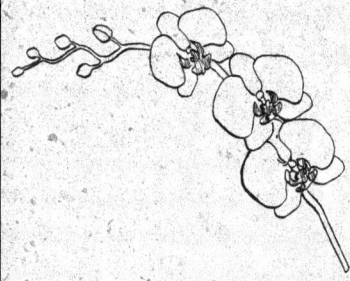

I have always been told that I could not understand.
What it takes to really be a man.
A life of trying to be strong
When it was easier to toke a bong.
At my funeral will there be songs?
Where they talk about what I did wrong?
Will they truly miss me when I am finally gone?

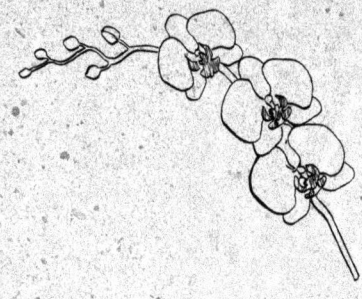

What will happen at the end?

When there is no love left to send?

Expressionless meetings were the beginning.

This is the case when something special is ending.

The hate is in control and spreading.

To the place where you are no longer living.

How I miss the little things.

A cloud floating in the clear spring sky.

A valley with a bright moon watching a raven fly.

The wilting leaves every fall.

A time when we gave it our all.

A wedding picture in an abandoned hall.

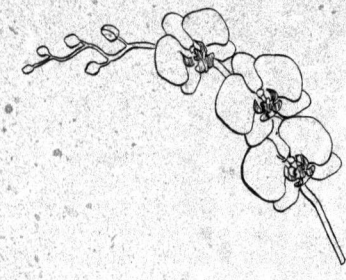

Remember the old days of our youth.
Turning in to something as worthless as phone booth.
We would be friends until we die.
Yet this ended like a young muscian's suicide.
A time that lips whispered lies.

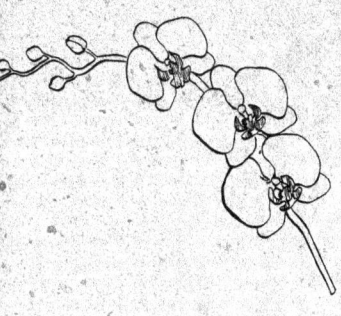

I already dream of the days our lives together will end.
You saved me from the the pits of myself friend.
I feel the warmth of a world I dream about in your eyes
I know you saved me from the worst times.
From using the leash to say good bye.

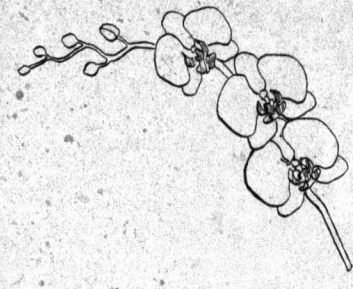

I speak to you quite often now.
How I miss those days of not long ago.
The days I wish I would of told you more.
Instead of acting like it was a chore.
My heart is lost and can never forget..
That these actions of mine have given my heart never-ending regret.

In a world of black and white.
Where what is never wrong or right.
It is the nature's songbird that sings at night.
The reason you get up every morning and fight.
In some beds they wish before darkness comes they see a white light.

The love that we live is sometimes a lie.
A break from the monotony then you become blind.
A depressed soul living in the dark.
The noose around their neck will definitely leave a mark.
Leaving what's most important behind.

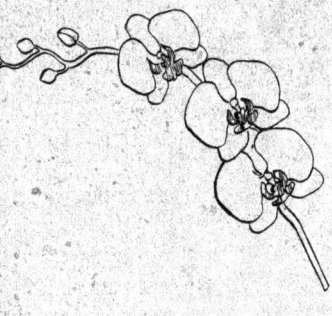

Hello, welcome back friend.
I see you need somone to torment.
An excuse for another experiment.
Travelled from a happy place you did?
You are only here to see my fucking end..

Am I terrified of the unexplained?
What is wrong with this brain?
No matter how damn hard I try
I cant forget when you said goodbye.
Following the the foot steps of the insane..

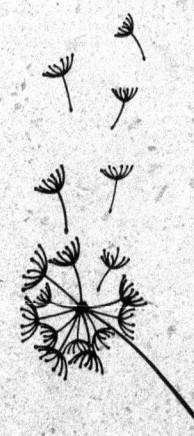

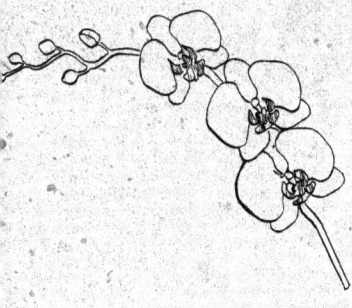

What is the use of disguising your fate?
What will you do when its too late?
Will you hope that it makes true sense?
Or will you not care and be fucking dense?
You have to let go of all of your hate.

Am I different, am I the best?
These are your feelings not a damn contest.
How do most go through out the day?
When you have taken everything how can I pay?
How do I separate this from the rest?

Sometimes we want to be seen.
A little respect from another human being.
Climb eveything that stands in our way.
To rest our ears on the chest where our hearts lay.
To scream louder than any fiend.

Young adult roams earth.
Acceptance
can make or break you.

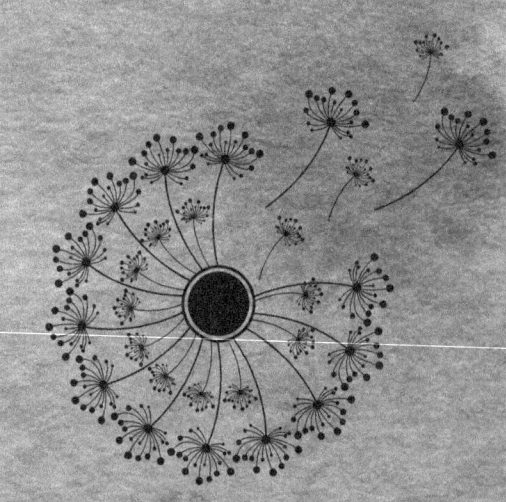

There is so much for you to see.
How I wish we could for a brief moment speak.
To beg forgiveness again even though I repented.
I try to walk again, but my mind has left to a world of the demented.
The journey ends for I am too weak.

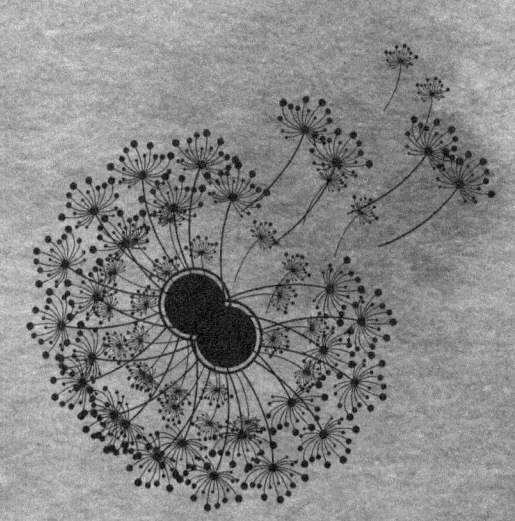

Love was always wanted
Or acceptance of how they were made.
Virtually in every teen's dreams.
Eventually paranoia turns to hate.

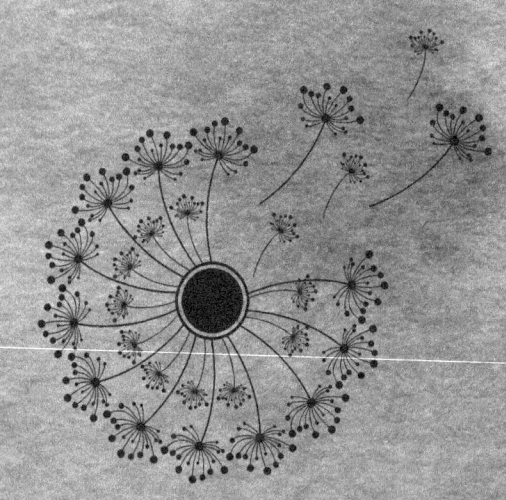

Quiet moments before the alarm rings
Under the sheets something is half dead.
Is this how the rest is going to be?
Even the air feels the same.
In the washing machine go
The dreams we searched for.
Letting us know
Yes it is never going to change.

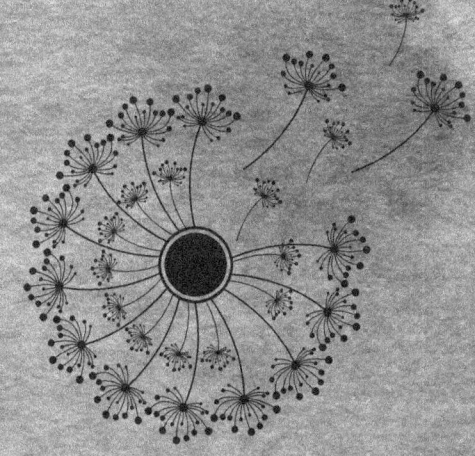

Mother where can I find comfort?
Or is this how it is going to be?
The street painter paints the eiffell tower.
How is this even a memory?
Eating at mcdonalds a little boy smiles.
A little blood drops on the autopsy room floor tiles.

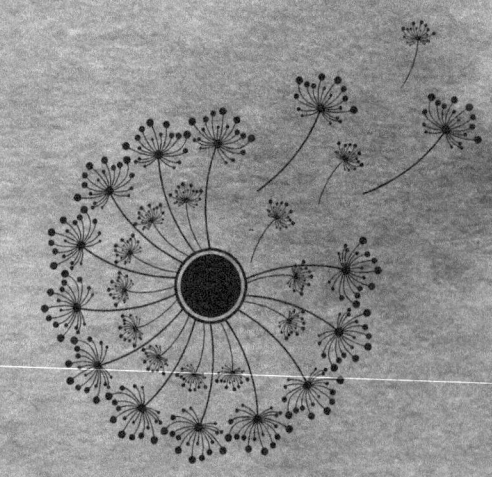

Forget the things that do not matter.
As fathers go you were all that I had.
These moments make me quite sad.
How I wish I could of told you more
Regret is the only feeling I have right now.

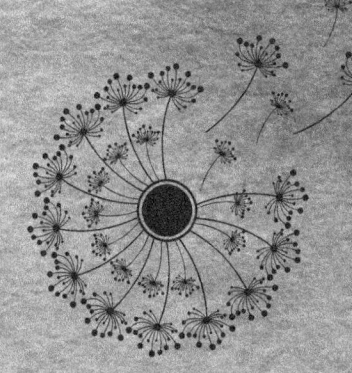

Great moments from long ago.
Really just triggers to remind me I'm old.
Eating more than I should when
Engaging in a fucked up world's survival.
Drinking to forget about the change in rules.

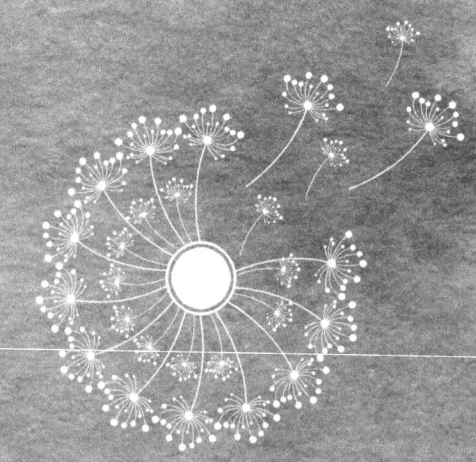

Relishing the moments before telling me
About the feelings long gone and your heart was free.
I didnt want to let you go.
Even though you hurt me so.
Hidden under clouds I couldnt see.

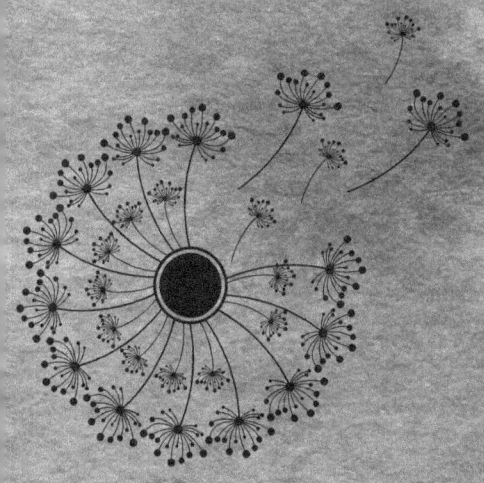

Gifts lost under a sea of tears.
The love you gave faded over years.
A blue sky forgottten in a world of grey.
Each wound a new lesson learned each day.
A well written script for an adoloscent's fears.

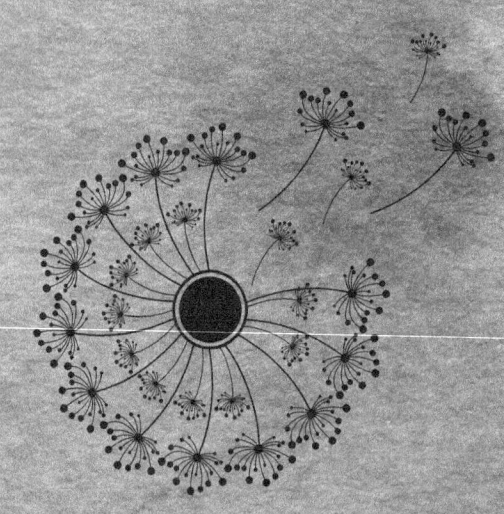

Yellow petals spread all over a church ground.
Death follows everyone around.
Taking away all thats precious.
Making my heart so malicious
To know my heart is truly found.

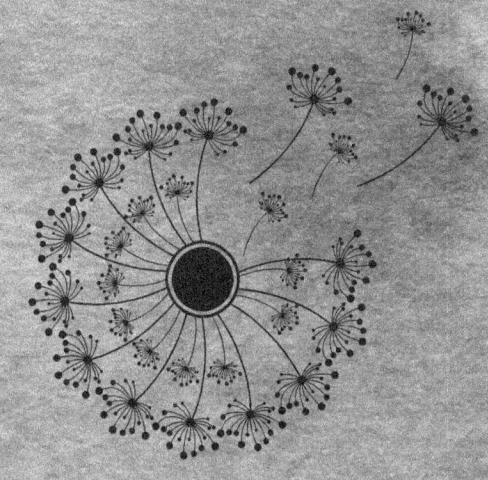

Goodbye to sunny days.
How I miss your touch and stare.
To not remember this would never be fair.
Waiting for someone to really care.
Love is an all in gamble if you dare.

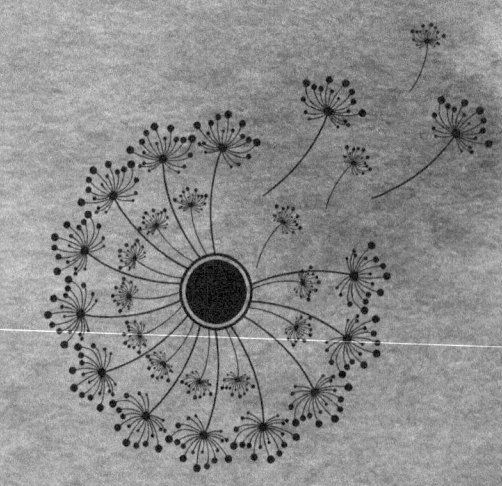

Washing away tears
As my soul obliterates pain.
Nothing broken left.

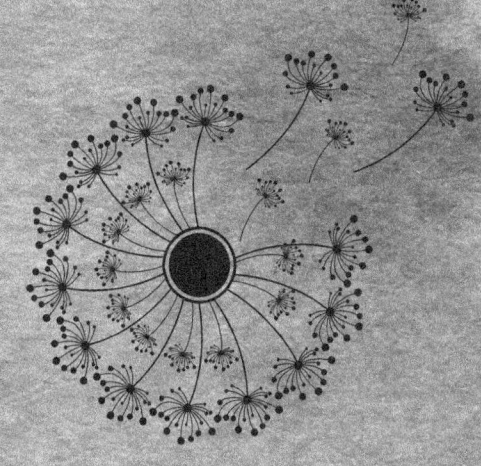

Willows in the spring
Mixed with cool rippling waters
Sadness reflecting.

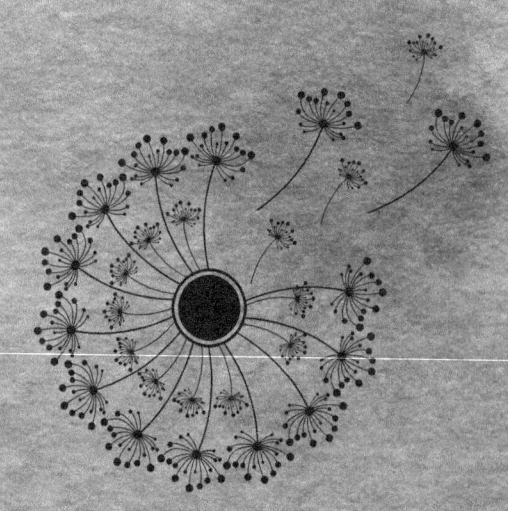

Mother
Will I let go?
Pain teases this old soul.
I want to see you when I can
Go home.

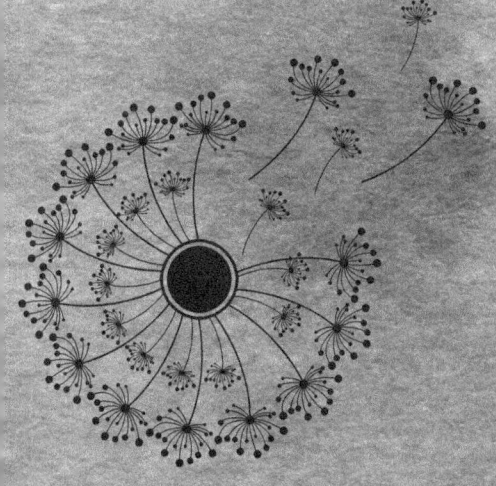

Where have
The sunny days gone?
How can I release pain
If I ignore every voice of
reason?

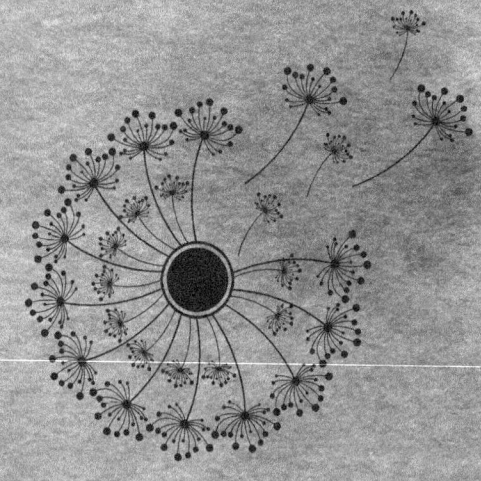

Painful
Are the moments
Delicate seconds lost.
Happiness remembered with such regret.

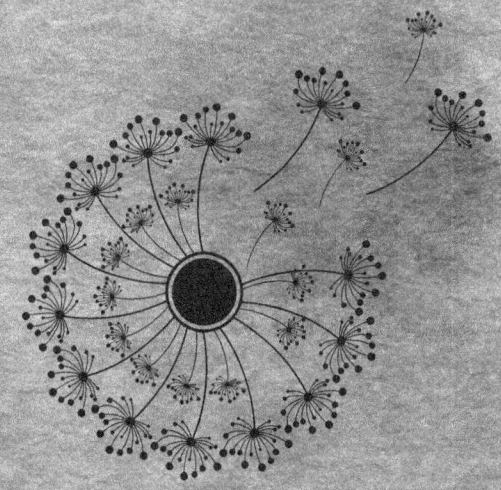

Blossoms
Sometimes brings hope.
After months of grief.
Rainbows camouflaging deceit.
Each time.

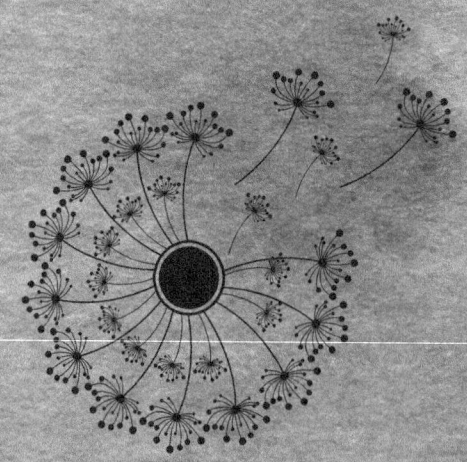

Slight autumn fever
Chills under warm blankets
Halloween sickness.

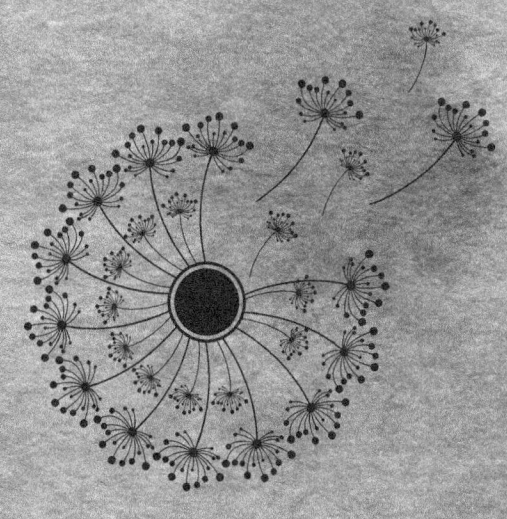

Old church bells ringing
On a cold rainy sunday
A funeral waits.

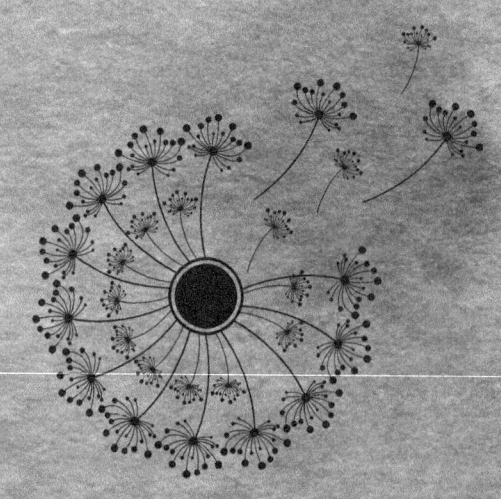

Tired of watching
The years slip away fading
In to memories.

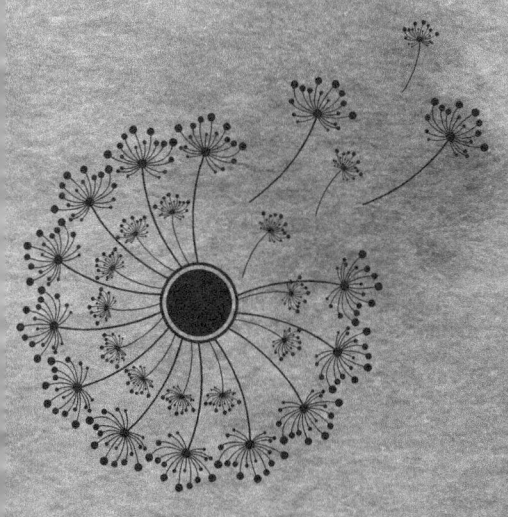

Up and fucking down
A rollercoaster of thoughts
Driven in the ground.

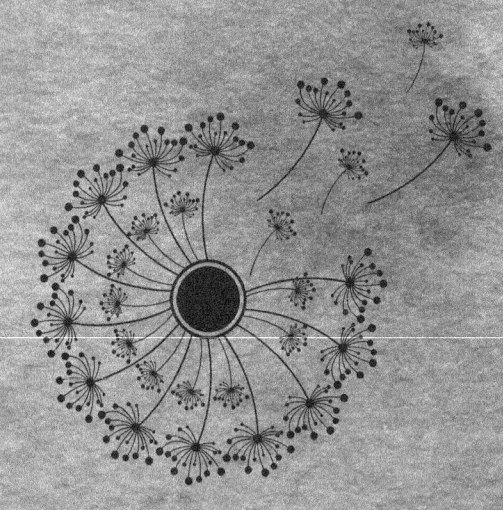

Pieces of my heart
Scattered from the raging storm
Windless change begins.

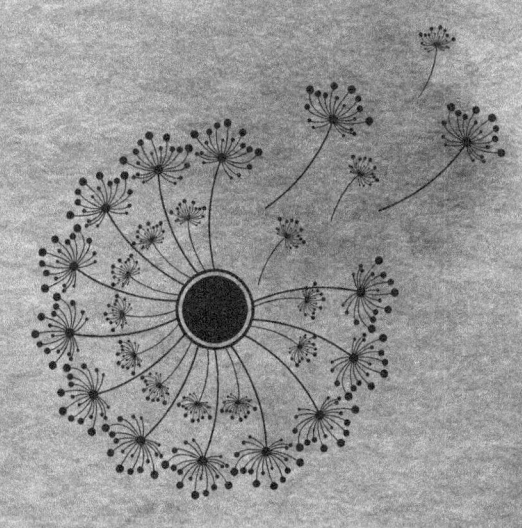

Darkest clouds bellow
Such Rage fills an empty heart
When a corpse appears.

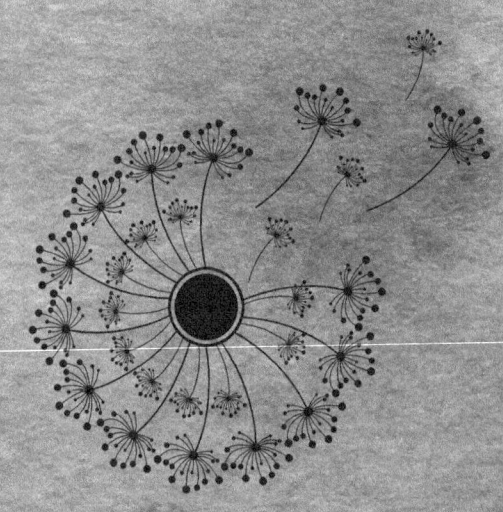

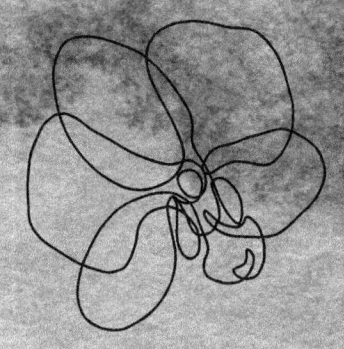

Where will I finally go?
Will I rest or scream, I want to know.
I Do not fear the nothingness of death.
I will love you until my last breath.
I will watch you grow old from below.

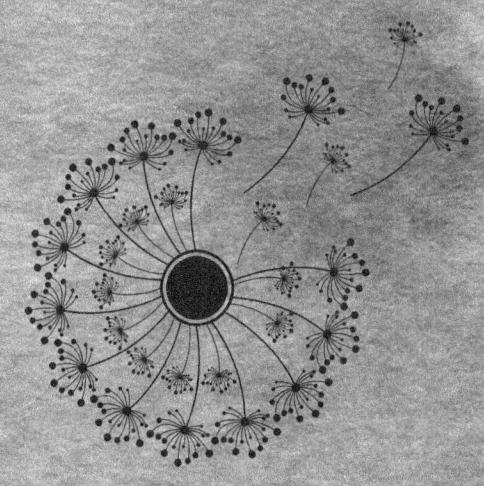

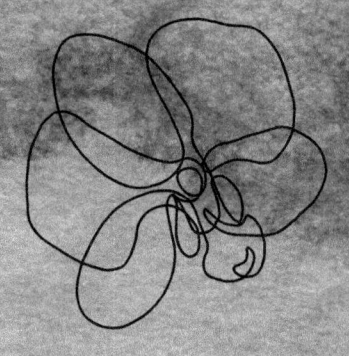

You loved me since my birth.
You were the only thing that loved me on this earth.
All of the gray in my hair.
Out to the dark cold sea I stare.
Deep inside I know I have no worth.

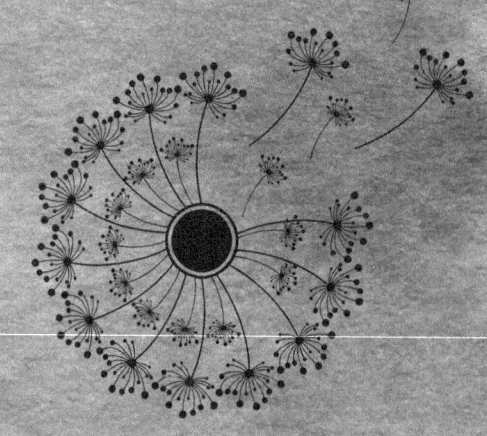

Stinging my very eyes
Tears of pain from many lives.
Every night they cry
Wishing that I would die
My heart is dead driving me to suicide.

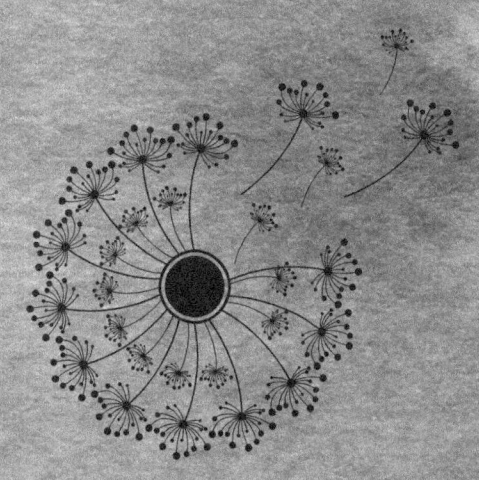

*Those trivial things
do matter.
Ask some divorcees.*

I can't seem to go on.
When the heart receives no nourishment.
Always lying in the bed.
Since the life of yesterday is now dead.
Some people may worry.
Hoping to stop the pain thats brewing.

Everywhere I go you follow.
From the rice in my cabinet
To creamer I place in my coffee I think of you.
I knew you would leave before me that is life.
Now I write down the pictures in my brain.
Of a life where we are together again.
Where colors exist not from the deepest pits of regret.

Hating
being always
weak, instead of taking
back what was mine in the fucking
first place.

Where is
the chemistry?
The flame of some desire.
To sacrifice one's happiness
for love.

What will I do now?
Where is the peace I search for?
A long way from home in a old world.
Scared of failing again.
To see the disappointment on my mother's face.
To know I threw away what was left.
Hoping for the better and cherishing what time is left.

It cuts through any steel.
The words of an ex lover
Hanging you like a noose.
Triggering many memories.
Some we run from and some deserve a good old tip of a hat.

How does love turn to hate?
Is divorce a clean slate?
Will I find love or is it too late?
If this was chess, you lost checkmate.
Dont cry standing on a crate
Maybe this is your only voice and fate.

Bloody fingers paint
on a tattered old canvas.
An old bride weeping..

Forget the madness.
Or the love that brought ruins.
Reach for every star.
On your way to some heaven.
Or park with singing love birds.

In my heart I see
Only one huge maze of thorns
Before my orchid.

An old cracked ceiling.
Eyes staring at each crevasse.
A slow drip echoes.

Love is like a beach
Beautiful and attracts all
Gazing thinkers.

Where can I bury this hate?
Of a life, I wish I could reset.
Let the words of children long ago disappear.
To a world where I truly matter.
Where my tears will be seen.
Not a used piece paper in a storm drain.
A moment to finally laugh
Instead of hours of staring in silence.
A life for some, instead of a dream my thoughts have spun.

Will you cry when I am only a memory.
Will you remember the moments we had.
Of a time long ago.
When two lives were shared.
A journey some will never make.
A risk that some will never take.
A love that they can never feel
A love that you know is truly real.
A drop of water that refuses to sink.
A myth or legend is what the wise men think.

As my eyes grow weary.
I fear how the time has changed me.
Sucked the life out of my being.
Knowing the best is gone.
How does one look at themself?
Seeing the smooth now wrinkled.
What was the deepest black is now mixed with gray.
I fear the unknown since this could be the last day.
If it is, I definitely know it is ok.

They say it is better to be late than never.
Yet they say what you dont know can't hurt you either.
I learned late and sacrficed so they wouldn't know.

Where am I now?
Should I be scared?
As I carefully walk through these meadows.
Searching for the way
Even though my heart chooses to stay.
Cherishing the time given.
Losing ourselves each day.
Where is my purpose now, I'm afraid.

We shall part soon.
I feel you at noon.
Consuming my whole day.
Would you love me if I stay?
Will you remember me during this time?
Will you miss the time we had?
Was it good or was it fucking bad?
I am nothing like your dad.
The black and white is quite dead.

Many tattered dreams
Soaking in the midnight rain
Memories in graves.

Songs of sirens
A World of such deception
Loving misery.

As each day passes,
Memories tease my Existence.
Reminding me I still live
And we wont laugh again.

Unfair
Or unlucky?
Does not really matter
When you search to erase all your
Regret

It hurts
Everyday still.
A world filled with ashes
Of lives thrown away, a fool to
Replace.

Screaming from the pain
Swallows try to fly away
Rain covers their wings.

Under the cold dark autumn nights.
I remember the patterns of our breath under the moonlight.
Many whispers from the wind filled our ears.
The eyes crossed leaves of gold and red.
The trees look withered and dead.
How I smiled thinking I had forever.
Now decades later my mind is the only thing left of yesterday.
Now I wait for my message from the sea.
I search for the perfect tree , where you can bury me.

Before the ride ends.

Beautiful

moments reappear.

Artists

On the boardwalk

Peforming all their tricks

A distant sun slowly setting

Will rest.

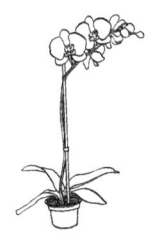

Three years have gone by.
In my mind it went quickly as a blink of an eye.
Yet my heart has slowly broken apart.
Everyday is quite the same.
Where I am the one to blame.
They say time will slowly heal.
Yet I only know this constant pain is real.
Where loss is the only thing I feel.

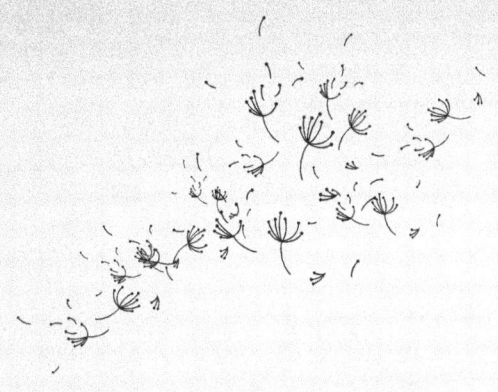

Do you
Remember the
Days when you could converse
With out it being a fucking
Contest?

Laughing
Yet still praying
For a final escape.
A vacation where you stay heart
Broken.

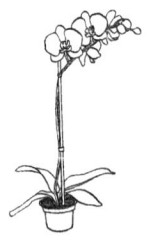

Mazes.

Confusing thoughts.

Losing our destiny.

Separated from our fate and

Not know.

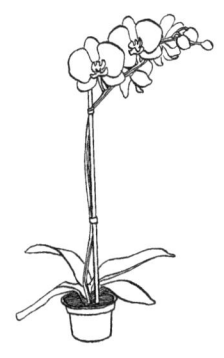

Tired,

So exhausted.

Feelings deterioate.

Barely floating in life is quite

Painful.

Loyal
Beyond belief.
Expressions of pure love.
I wouldnt trade this for anything.
Canines.

Why was I weak?
During those years what did you seek?
You waited until the gray filled our hair.
Did you ever care?
Now for hours I stare
At a door probaby leading nowhere.
A pretty note left on a chair.
A dangerous game we all play if we dare.

Crisscrossing patterns
Light up the clear autumn sky
Reflecting off eyes.

Kiss me one last time.
reminding me what I will miss
When I'm fucking dead.

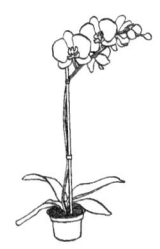

Loving you killed me.
Ripping my soul from these bones
Leaving only old.

An old man passes the torch.
Trying to remember was it worth it.
Chasing himself through the years.
Always was quite deaf , when it came to advice.
Chasing the dream in a fool's world.
Staring at his empty glass while he smokes his last cigarette.

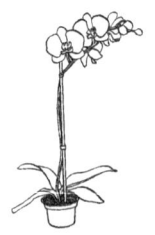

Where have you been?
I have missed you my friend.
Times have become clear.
What was once beautiful has become rotten.
Words from some pretty famous authors
Have placed themselves inside my brain.
Now when I look nothing seems the same.
Another wish for the tooth fairy another Sunday school prayer.
A logical reason to remove the layer that separates us.

Crooked as a bend
Arthritic fingers jam away
Guitar case with change.

Heavy as a freight train
Yet it never moves
Crushing every moment
I think of them.
Was I worthy to have ever known them.
Probably not or I wouldn't regret it.

There is never a clean slate
If there is I can't relate.
Some questions asked are never too late.
Words of wisdom written on scrolls
Piled under an old staircase
A child sits alone in the corner when they can't dream anymore.

Perhaps we all will find it.
Even if it is when we are old.
Another reason to get up in the morning.
Cherished moments told by campfires.
Evenings where songs were sung ,a time remembered.

Porcelain dolls sit
On an old forgotten chest
A child remembers.

Looking past the deception of older folks.
Wanting us to follow their set of rules.
While they are the ones that look like fools.
People spend years to find their own zen
These idiots can change your life with the stroke of a pen.
Wouldn't life be more grand with a fucking competent government.

I dream of a set of parents with their two children.
Splitting them down the middle, a cut like halves of a cake.
The times of yesterday , where the smell of fresh bread filled the air.
Flashbacks are now quite cruel since everyone,but me is dead.
I wonder when they were up late at night, what did they think about.
When your time is near and you have access to a pen.
Would your last words be the rambling of person noone can comprehend?.

A thousand words hide.

Moments of ago captured.

Painters imitate.

I envy this bridge

we will be reunited

Happy as rainbows.

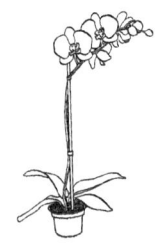

Forgive them before death.
Remember only the best.
Truly live before you too are dead.

Music from master
Crows flying across valleys
A present from death.

Hiding silently

mouse raises its little head

Cats watch patiently.

"In a world of Black and White" where darkness covers the canvas everywhere I look.

A dream a child wants instead of a land of hurt. If God created us equally, why do others smile when I frown?

Why do I lack the energy to get out of bed? When will these years of depression come to an end?

There is no sunshine in these pages, but every word needs to be said.

I find sharing these thoughts to be better than any medicine.

I wish for the stars, but I hope my words can comfort some before I am dead.

www.ingramcontent.com/pod-product-compliance
Lightning Source LLC
Chambersburg PA
CBHW062040290426
44109CB00026B/2681